THE HUMAN MACHINE

MOVERS
AND *SHAPERS*

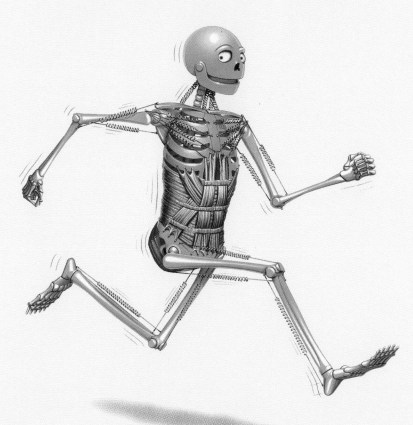

Sarah Angliss

Illustrations by Tom Connell

Thameside Press

Distributed in the United States by
Smart Apple Media
123 South Broad Street
Mankato, Minnesota 56001

Text copyright © Sarah Angliss 1999

Editor: Susie Brooks
Designer: Helen James
Educational consultant: Carol Ballard

Printed in Singapore

ISBN 1-929298-18-8
Library of Congress Catalog Card Number 99-73412

10 9 8 7 6 5 4 3 2 1

Words in **bold** are explained in the glossary on pages 30 and 31.

CONTENTS

MOVERS AND SHAPERS

Think of your body as an amazing machine— a human machine. Think of your skeleton and muscles as a strong, flexible framework. They hold the machine up, protect the delicate parts inside it, and enable it to move around.

Skeleton scaffold

Most of your body parts are soft and floppy, but you have a firm, definite shape. That's because you have a skeleton—a set of hard and fairly rigid bones. Your bones are your shapers. They hold up your body parts and give them some protection.

Moving muscles

Your skeleton wouldn't be much use without muscles—your movers. Muscles tug on the bones they're attached to and force them to change their position. Your movers and shapers work together constantly, enabling you to stand up, move around, sit still—or simply lie down.

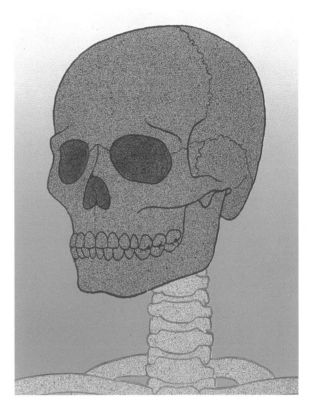

Funny figures

Your muscles and bones aren't really made of springs and plastic. The central illustrations in this book are drawn with a bit of imagination—but they do explain the different jobs that your movers and shapers can do. Diagrams like the one above reflect more closely how things actually look.

Breakdown!

Just like the working parts of any other machine, your movers and shapers can break down. Some parts can mend themselves, but others may need a helping hand. Toolboxes like this one tell you what happens when your moving framework needs repair.

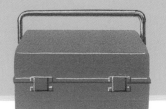

5

SUPER SHAPERS

The human machine's movable frame is called a skeleton. It's made of many different-shaped pieces. These are your bones.

Take a look at the shape of your body. Some parts are long and thin, others are short or bumpy. Because your framework is made up of so many different kinds of parts, it can bend and twist in a great variety of ways.

You can think of your skeleton as a construction kit that contains various types of bones. These two pages tell you about the different pieces that make it up.

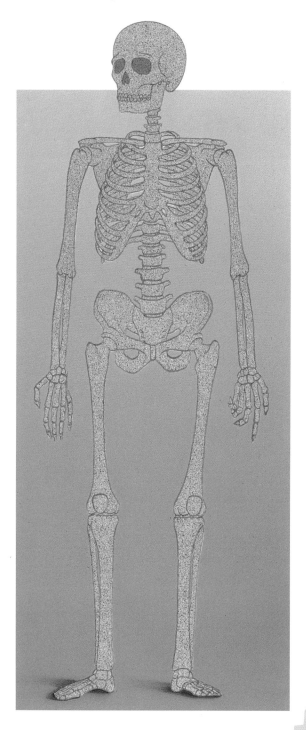

Long bones

These are like long, thin rods with bulging ends. You find them in your arms and legs.

Short bones

These bones are shaped like small blocks. You have many of them in your wrists and ankles.

Irregular bones

These are bones that don't fit into any of the other groups. They come in many odd shapes and include your **vertebrae**, hip bones, and some of the bones in your face.

What's your number?

Babies are born with more than 300 separate bones, but most adults have only 206. That's because as you grow, many small bones fuse together to form larger ones (see page 17, for example). Amazingly, over half the bones in your body are found in your hands and feet.

BONE KIT

Round bones

These cover and protect some delicate **joints**. Your kneecaps are the largest round bones in your body.

How do your bones fit together? Find out on pages 12–13.

Spare parts

Just like your skin, most bones heal if they're broken (see page 27). But occasionally a person may damage a bone so badly that it won't mend properly. When this happens, surgeons may have to replace it with an artificial body part made of plastic or a lightweight metal that won't rust or irritate the body.

Flat bones

Some flat bones, such as your ribs, are narrow and curvy. Others are more like plates. They include the bones in your upper skull.

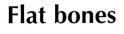

MIGHTY MOVERS

*T*he human frame
is covered with over
650 muscles. Some are
stronger than others, but most
muscles tug on your body to
keep you upright or in action.

If you look closely at athletes' bodies, you'll
see the outlines of their muscles bulging under
their skin. Your skeleton is covered with muscles
that make up nearly half of your bodyweight.

Pulling power

Most muscles work by pulling on your bones.
They're attached by tough strings, called **tendons**,
which hook on to bony knobs, called **processes**.

On command from your brain, a muscle will
shorten, or **contract**. The shortened muscle tugs
on the bone it's attached to, forcing it to move.

Many muscles

Skeletal muscles are adjusting their length all
the time, creating the forces you need to stay
upright, move, and pick things up. They all work
in the same way, but they vary in their size and
strength. Your large, strong thigh muscles, for
example, support your weight and help you to
walk. Your smaller, weaker hand muscles let you
make controlled, delicate movements.

Main front muscles

biceps relaxes

triceps contracts

biceps contracts

triceps relaxes

Double act

Almost all your muscles
work in pairs. As one tightens,
its partner relaxes. If you squeeze
your upper arm gently as you bend your
elbow, you'll feel a pair of muscles in action.
The **biceps**, on top of your arm, tightens up,
while the **triceps**, on the underside, relaxes.

Winter warmer

When a muscle's working hard,
it makes lots of heat. That's why
you feel warmer if you walk fast
or run. When you're very cold,
your brain forces your muscles to
change length hundreds of times
a minute, giving you the shivers.
This helps to warm you up.

What makes a
muscle contract?
Find out on page 11.

When you straighten your arm, these
muscles work in reverse. Your triceps
contracts, while your biceps relaxes.

Acid alarm

*If a muscle gets overworked, it
soon lets you know. It floods with
lactic acid—a liquid that makes it
ache. Your muscles always release
this acid when they work. It usually
drains away into your bloodstream,
but an overworked muscle can't
clear it away fast enough. When
a muscle starts
to hurt, you
know it's time
to take a rest.*

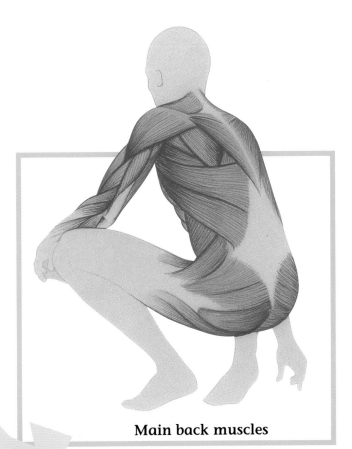

Main back muscles

STRONG STUFF

Movers and shapers are made of strong stuff. They're also carefully put together so they can support your body and keep it balanced.

Balancing act

Your skeleton is bottom-heavy to make you stable. A broad bony beam, called your **pelvis**, spreads your weight evenly between both legs. Your feet are arched to make them strong enough to carry you.

Muscles all over your body help to keep you steady. They tug on your bones in just the right sequence to stop you from toppling over.

Bare bones

Bones are strong but light because they're built in two layers. They have a dense coating of **compact bone**, composed of hard, tightly-packed cylinders. This surrounds your **spongy bone**, which is very light because it's full of little spaces, like a honeycomb.

Just like concrete, your bones contain two main ingredients, **calcium** and **collagen**, which combine to make them strong.

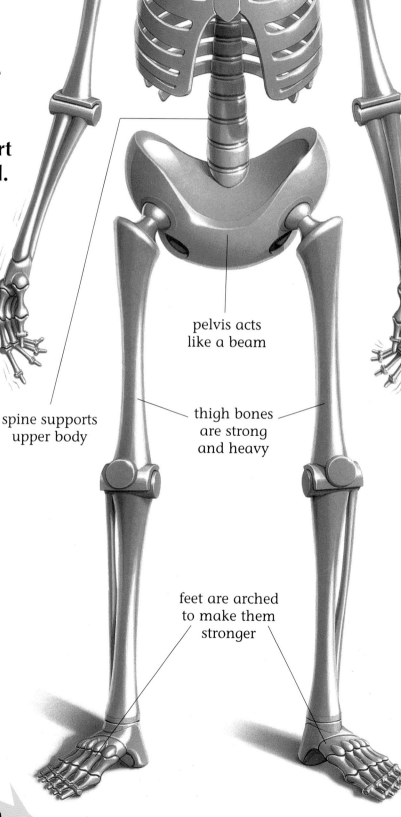

pelvis acts like a beam

spine supports upper body

thigh bones are strong and heavy

feet are arched to make them stronger

10

Soft centers

Although you may not think it, your bones are full of life. Your blood constantly brings them supplies of **oxygen** and **nutrients** to feed their **cells**.

A soft jelly, called **marrow**, fills the center of each long bone and the spaces in your spongy bone. There are two types of marrow. Yellow marrow stores some of your body's fat. Red marrow makes and stores many of your body's blood cells.

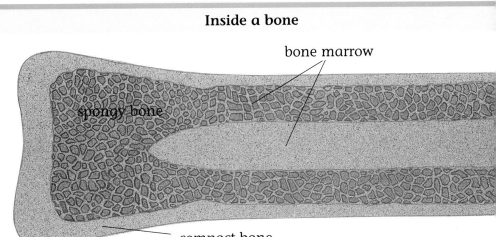

Inside a bone

bone marrow

spongy bone

compact bone

Muscle make-up

A muscle is tough and bendable because it's made of thousands of tiny **fibers**, just like a rope. Every fiber is made of hundreds of even finer threads, called **myofibrils**. A single myofibril is very weak, but lots of them bundled together make a strong band of muscle.

Room for growth

Baby bones are much softer than adult ones. That's because they contain lots of **cartilage**. This slightly springy stuff allows your bones to grow and change shape. As you grow up, the cartilage turns into hard bone. Most people's bones don't harden completely until they're about 25 years old.

Super sliders

The moving parts of a muscle are minute strands of **protein**, called **filaments**. In a relaxed muscle, these strands lie almost end to end—but on command from your brain they can slide right over one another, bunching up into a pile. This makes each myofibril shorter and fatter, forcing the whole muscle to **contract**.

Filaments lock together as you clench a muscle. When you want to relax it, they slide apart again, returning the muscle to its original length.

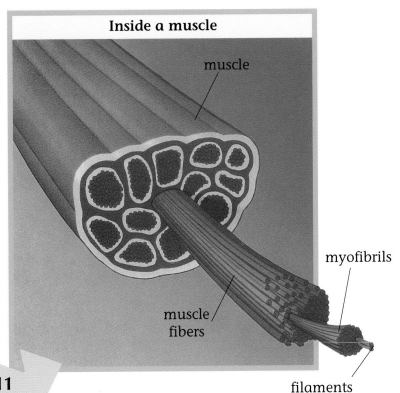

Inside a muscle

muscle

myofibrils

muscle fibers

filaments

MOVING PARTS

Your shapers fit together at places called joints. These work in many different ways so you can bend, twist, or straighten your body.

Scissors, cranes, and doorknobs all have simple **joints**—parts that turn or slide around each other. The human machine is far more flexible than any of these. Your joints allow your body to move in a great variety of ways.

Hinge joints

These joints move back and forth on a single plane, like the hinge of a door. You have a hinge joint in each of your elbows and knees.

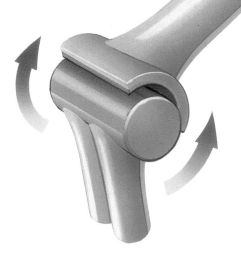

A few of your joints hardly move at all. See some of them on pages 14–15.

Pivot joints

These joints enable body parts to swivel around a central point, like a swinging garden gate. Pivot joints are located in your wrists and ankles.

Ball-and-socket joints

These joints can turn in almost any direction—just like the joystick of a computer game. You have these joints in your hips and shoulders.

Smooth swiveling

Your bones would wear away if they rubbed together at your joints. That's why each one has its own cushion of **cartilage** protecting it like a rubber washer. A slimy liquid called **synovial fluid** oils your joints by forming a thin layer between bones to reduce friction.

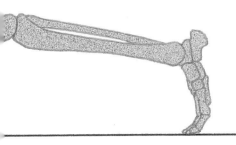

Saddle joints

The bones in these joints move around as if they were rocking in a saddle. You have joints like this at the base of each thumb.

Gliding joints

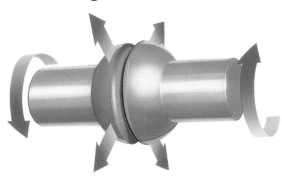

In these joints the flat surfaces of bones can slide over each other a little—in almost any direction. You'll find gliding joints between your **vertebrae** and in your ankles and wrists.

Wear and tear

*Your joints are held together by straps called **ligaments**, which help keep your bones from popping out of place. If you've ever suffered a **sprain**, you've probably stretched a ligament too far, or even torn it. When this happens, your joint fills with extra synovial fluid for protection, making it puffy and stiff. You may have to rest it until the fluid drains away.*

BRAIN BOX

sutures join skull bones

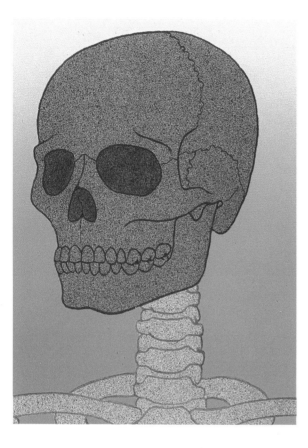

Your brain is your control center. It requires a tough protective casing, which is your skull. Covering this strong box are many muscles that move your face.

Helmet head

The top part of your skull, the **cranium**, acts like a built-in crash helmet to stop you from bruising your brain when you bump your head.

The cranium consists of eight bones that fit together perfectly, like curving jigsaw pieces. Their zigzag-shaped edges meet at **joints** called **sutures**, which are fixed so they can hardly move at all.

Face base

The front of your skull gives shape to your face and is made up of 14 bones. These include ridged parts that stick out like bumpers to protect your eyes.

Your lower jaw bone, or **mandible**, is your skull's only moving part. It wiggles in many directions so you can talk or chew.

Smart cycling

Your skull is a good protector for your brain—but it does have its limits. If you fall and your head hits hard ground, you may crack one of your cranial bones. A really bad fall may even damage your brain. That's why it's good to wear a helmet when cycling or skateboarding. A helmet adds an extra layer of protection to your brain box, keeping your control center as safe as possible.

fluid inside skull
cushions brain

Face space

Two small bones form the bridge of your nose, but the pointed part is made from **cartilage**. This sticks out from a hole in your skull. Other holes in your skull make space for your eyes and ears. Inside each ear there are three of the tiniest bones in your body.

Hollows in the bones around your nose, called **sinuses**, help make your head lighter and easier to carry. Sinuses are joined by openings to the airway in your nose.

Express yourself

Your face is covered with a network of muscles that pull its skin around like a rubbery sheet. These muscles help you to smile, look puzzled, or frown.

Your eyelids have the fastest-working muscles in your body. They make you blink about 20,000 times a day, which protects your eyes and keeps them from drying out.

Main face muscles

lower jaw
moves around

Easy to smile

Smile then frown in front of a mirror to see how your face changes. When you smile, about 20 muscles contract, pulling up the corners of your mouth, raising your eyebrows, and opening your eyes wider. Looking grumpy is harder work. You need to contract over 70 muscles to frown.

SUPPLE SUPPORT

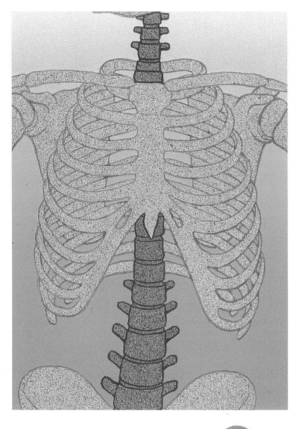

A narrow, bendable column—your spine—holds up your brain box and all your upper body parts. It's supported by a set of strong muscles in your

If you run your fingers down the center of your back, you'll feel a line of knobs. Each lump is part of a set of bones called **vertebrae** that slot together in a column to form your **spine**.

Your spine runs from the base of your skull to the bottom of your **pelvis**. Because it's made of so many tiny parts, it can bend in various ways. This enables you to touch your toes, twist around, or even curl up in a ball.

Curving column

Your spine is never perfectly straight—even when you stand up. It has gentle s-shaped curves that act like shock absorbers, allowing your spine to flex a little when you move. This helps to keep your bones from jarring together.

Weight lifters

Your spine and body muscles support a lot of weight, but they may be overstrained if they have to carry too much. You can harm your back by bending over to lift heavy loads—so always try to bend your knees, not your spine, when you pick up something extremely heavy.

Cartilage cushion

Your vertebrae can slide over each other slightly to let your spine move. Disks of springy **cartilage** cushion the surfaces where they meet, so the bones don't rub together and wear away. This cartilage squashes slightly as you bend.

Piecing together

A child has 33 vertebrae, but an adult has only 26. That's because as you grow up, the bottom nine vertebrae fuse to form two larger bones—your **sacrum** and **coccyx**.

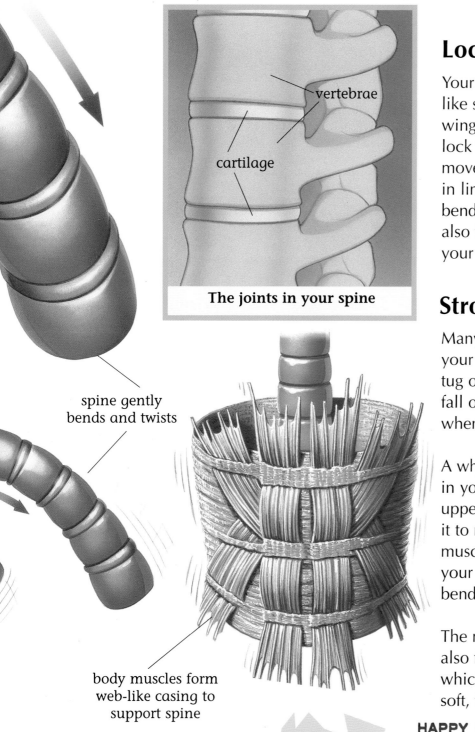

vertebrae

cartilage

The joints in your spine

spine gently bends and twists

body muscles form web-like casing to support spine

Locking links

Your vertebrae are shaped like small cylinders with bony wings. Some of these wings lock together as your spine moves. This keeps the column in line and stops it from bending too far. These knobs also form a protective cover for your delicate **spinal cord**.

Strong support

Many muscles work to support your spine. Those in your neck tug on your skull so it doesn't fall off its narrow perch—even when you lean right over.

A whole web of muscles in your **abdomen** keeps your upper body stable and enables it to move. You can feel these muscles working if you touch your front or sides when you bend or twist around.

The muscles of your **torso** also form a tough casing which protects the many soft, fragile organs inside.

SAFETY CAGE

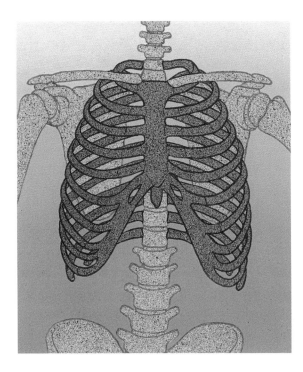

A movable cage creates ideal protection for the human power pack—your heart and lungs. It's made up of 12 pairs of curving bars, or ribs.

ribs curve around lungs

Breathing space

Every time you breathe, your **lungs** expand, then contract. Your **heart** changes shape as it beats. Your ribs form a cage that protects these important parts. This cage is hinged, so that it can move up and down as you breathe.

Roomy rack

You have 12 pairs of ribs. Ten pairs are attached to a flat plate at the front of your chest called your **sternum**. The lowest two pairs don't meet at the front at all. These are known as floating ribs.

Squashy **cartilage** joins your ribs to your sternum. This lets your ribcage shift a little as you move and breathe. At the back, each rib is joined to one of the **vertebrae** that make up your **spine**.

Always on the go

Throughout your lifetime, your ribcage will probably move more often than any other set of bones in your body. You take a breath about 12 times a minute—so your ribcage has to shift in and out around six million times a year!

Space makers

When you breathe in, a sheet-like muscle, called your **diaphragm**, pulls downward inside you. It squeezes everything below it, making room for your lungs to expand and take in air. As this happens, muscles in your **abdomen** push outward to make more space for your lower body parts.

At the same time, special muscles between your ribs, called **intercostal muscles**, work to expand your safety cage. They tighten to pull your ribs upward and outward and bring your sternum forward.

most ribs are joined to sternum

cartilage in joints lets ribcage move and expand

diaphragm moves up and down

ribs connect to vertebrae at back

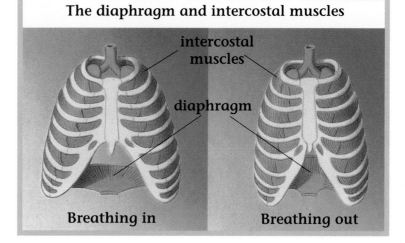

The diaphragm and intercostal muscles

intercostal muscles

diaphragm

Breathing in   Breathing out

Sore sides

*If you've ever had a sharp pain in your side, you may have suffered from a **cramp** in your diaphragm or intercostal muscles. Sometimes— during exercise, for example—these muscles **contract** sharply and tense up, which may be painful.*

GRABBERS AND GRIPPERS

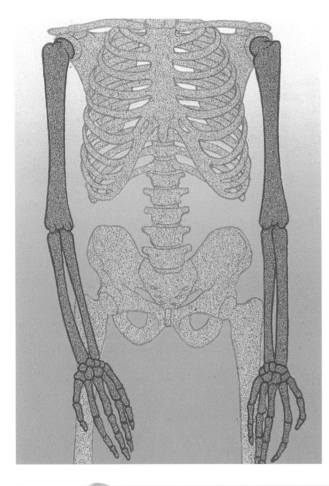

Two special cranes make it easy for the human machine to reach things, carefully pick them up, and move them. These are your arms and hands.

Great grabbers

Your arms meet your body at your shoulders. These ball-and-socket **joints** let you swing your arms around in almost any direction.

The bone in your upper arm, called your **humerus**, joins two lower arm bones, the **radius** and **ulna**, at your elbow. Your elbow has a hinge joint that you can bend. You are also able to twist your lower arm around, or move it from side to side.

Little grippers

You can wiggle your wrists, hands, and fingers in all sorts of ways because they're made up of many small jointed parts.

Your wrist is both a gliding joint and a hinge made up of eight small bones. There are five bones in your palm, three in each of your fingers, and two in your thumb. The many joints in your hands enable you to wrap them tightly around objects of all different shapes.

Popping out

We often reach out our arms to break a fall—but they can't always take the strain. A heavy tumble could **dislocate** your shoulder or elbow, forcing the bones in the joint to pop out of place. This happens when the **ligaments** aren't strong enough to hold the bones firmly together.

hands and
wrists move
in many ways

Double trouble

How far can you bend back your
thumb without forcing it? A few people
can easily make their thumbnail touch
their arm. We call people who are this
flexible double-jointed. They're often
good at gymnastics, playing musical
instruments, and other things that
make the most of really flexible
joints—but they're also more
likely to suffer **sprains**.

shoulder has
ball-and-socket
joint

lower arm has
two bones

elbow has
hinge joint

strap-like
ligaments
hold joints
together

Strong or sensitive

The muscles in your grabbers
and grippers are all good for
different jobs. Large muscles in
your arms, such as your **biceps**
and **triceps**, give you strength
to lift things or to reach out.

Your hands and wrists have
a much finer set of muscles that
make them strong enough to
grip something tightly, gentle
enough to pick up fragile
objects, and supple enough
to play an instrument.

String-like **tendons** run from
muscles in your arms to your
palms and fingers. These let
you bend your fingers or
spread out your hands.

**Find out more
about joints
and ligaments
on pages 12–13.**

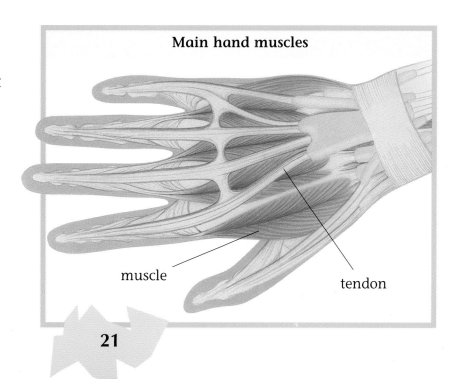

Main hand muscles

muscle

tendon

21

STURDY SEAT

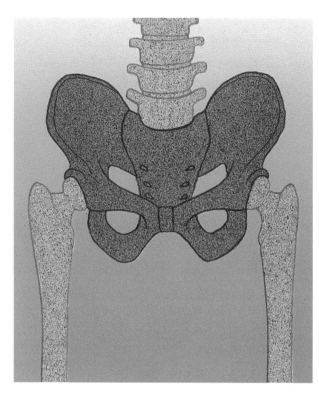

A heavy beam of bone, called the pelvis, forms a strong seat for every human machine. It's covered with large muscles that help make sitting comfortable.

A chair must be strong enough to take the weight of your body. So must your **pelvis**—the bone that you sit on. Your pelvis is shaped a bit like a bottomless bowl. It's made of two large, curved bones that are fused to either side of your **sacrum**—the triangular base of your **spine**.

Sitting comfortably

Only the underside of your pelvis meets the chair when you sit down. Fortunately it's padded with two large buttocks that spread the load as you sit. Each buttock has a huge, rounded muscle, called a **gluteus maximus**, that cushions a large part of your pelvis. When you wish to stand, each gluteus maximus contracts to bring your bottom forward and upward.

Shock absorber

A fused set of bones at the end of your spine forms your **coccyx**. When you sit down, this squashes a bit, like a spring, and absorbs some of the impact of your buttocks hitting the chair. This helps to stop you from jarring your back.

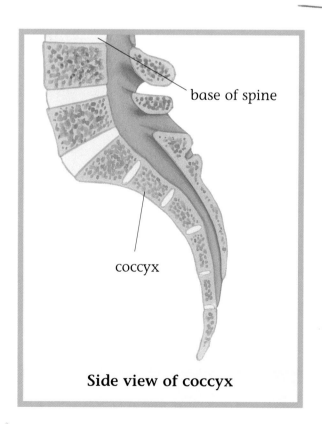

base of spine

coccyx

Side view of coccyx

22

pelvis is curved
like a bowl

Child friendly

A woman's pelvis is a slightly different shape
from a man's. It's usually broader and flatter,
with a wider opening in the middle. When
a woman gives birth, she has
to push out her new baby
through this opening.

ball-and-socket hip
joint lets leg move

Swinging sockets

The sides of your pelvis
form your hips. Your legs are
connected to your hips by
ball-and-socket **joints**. These
joints let you swing your legs
in many directions, so you
can walk and move around.

buttock muscles
cushion pelvis and
help you stand up

Wind and grind

*You use joints such as your hips so
often, they can eventually wear out.
Many people develop a condition
called **osteoarthritis** when they reach
old age. The **cartilage** that cushions
their joints wears thin, making the
bones grind together.
This makes the joints
swollen and painful.*

Tail end

According to many scientists, our
distant ancestors may have been
ape-like creatures with tails. As they
evolved into humans over millions
of years, their tails became shorter.
The coccyx we now have may
be a remnant of this tail.

SMOOTH STEPPERS

To take
a step:

turn pelvis

bend knees
and ankles

push off toes
to shift weight
from one foot
to other

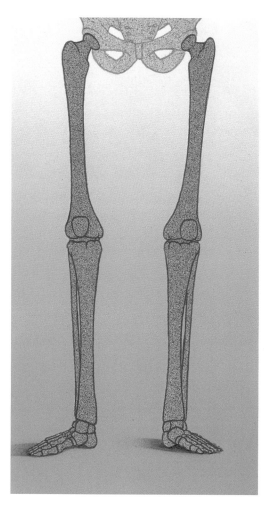

The human machine is unusual because it can balance easily on two legs— what's more, these legs can walk, skip, and run.

Think of all the things you need to do just to take one step. Walking uses every **joint**, muscle, and bone from your hips to your toes—and many upper body parts, too. These all work together, pushing you off one foot and shifting you forward slightly to move you, then putting down your other foot to keep you balanced.

Uneven walking

If you hurt one of your legs, you may develop an uneven walk, called a limp. This is your body's way of protecting the damaged part—it makes your other leg take more weight so the damaged one has a chance to heal.

Pushing power

The muscles in your legs and feet give you power to run and jump. Your strong thigh muscles work the hardest. They take most of your weight as you walk. Your lower leg muscles help move your feet to push you away from the ground.

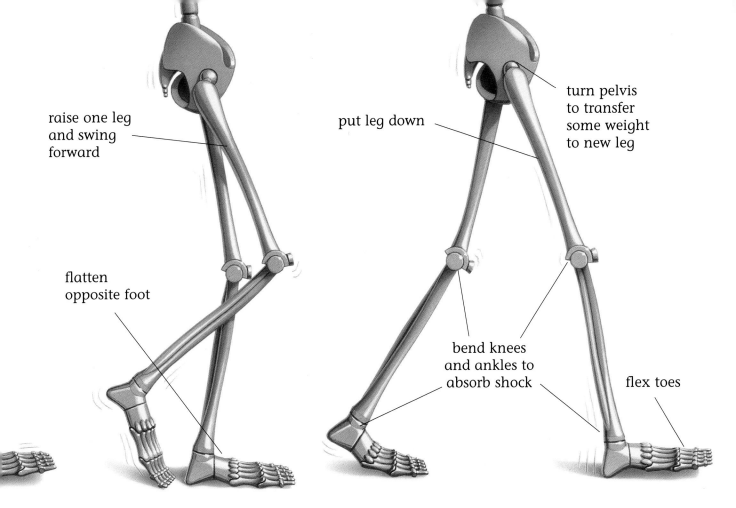

raise one leg and swing forward

flatten opposite foot

put leg down

turn pelvis to transfer some weight to new leg

bend knees and ankles to absorb shock

flex toes

Firm footing

Your feet are like platforms that are arched to make them strong. Your ankles allow them to move and twist around the ends of your legs. There are 28 bones in every foot and ankle. Because they're made up of so many parts, feet can change shape as you shift your weight between your heels and toes.

The knee joint

Your thigh bone, or **femur**, is the longest, strongest, and heaviest bone in your body. It joins two bones in your lower leg, the **tibia** and **fibula**, at your knee. Your knee is a powerful hinge joint that's protected by the kneecap, or **patella**.

Light landing

You usually bend your legs a little when you hit the ground after a jump. This is how you absorb some of the shock of landing. If your legs stayed straight, you would jar the rest of your body, especially your **spine**.

The knee joint

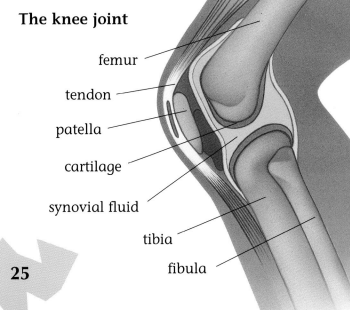

femur

tendon

patella

cartilage

synovial fluid

tibia

fibula

CARE AND SERVICING

Unlike most machines, the more you use your movers and shapers, the better they will work. But if you overstrain or damage them, you may need to have them repaired.

The best way to keep your bones and muscles in good working order is to exercise regularly and eat healthy meals.

Feeding your framework

Food that's rich in **calcium** helps to make your bones strong. Milk and cheese both contain lots of this. They also contain **protein**, which is good for building your muscles. You'll find protein in meats, nuts, and cereals, too.

If you eat plenty of these things while you're young, they'll help you form a framework that will last you for life.

joints can wear out or pop out of place

plaster casts hold broken bones in place

muscles and tendons can tear

bones can break in different ways

ankles can be sprained easily

Strength of the sun

Sunshine doesn't only make you feel warm—it can also strengthen your bones. That's because sunlight on your skin activates chemicals in your body that can make **vitamin D**. You need this to help your bones absorb and use **nutrients**.

Old bones

As you reach old age, your skeleton becomes weaker and more fragile. That's because your blood no longer brings your bones so many of the nutrients that keep them strong. The bones gradually become thinner and more spongy—they may even shrink in size. That's why some people become smaller or more stooped as they grow old.

Faulty frame

Sometimes you hurt your muscles or bones, perhaps by falling or by working them too hard. A good rest will usually heal a slight **sprain** or pulled muscle, but anything more serious may require a doctor.

Although your skeleton and muscles are hidden under your skin, doctors are still able to examine them. They can feel your muscles and **joints** to see if they are torn or sprained. But if they want to find out whether you've broken a bone, they'll probably take an **x-ray**.

Running repairs

Amazingly, a broken bone can repair itself. The living **cells** inside it work to heal the crack, using the nutrients and **oxygen** brought to them by your blood. Eventually enough new bone will grow to fuse the broken pieces together.

A plaster cast helps a bone to heal by keeping it stationary so it will fuse together properly. More serious breaks may require surgery to pin the pieces together.

How a bone mends

blood oozes out of broken bone and hardens in crack

cells start to make new spongy bone and marrow

new bone hardens to mend break

OTHER MODELS

Your muscles and skeleton are good at moving and shaping you—but the human machine is not the only model around. There are many different living creatures all over the world—and every one has tailor-made movers and shapers.

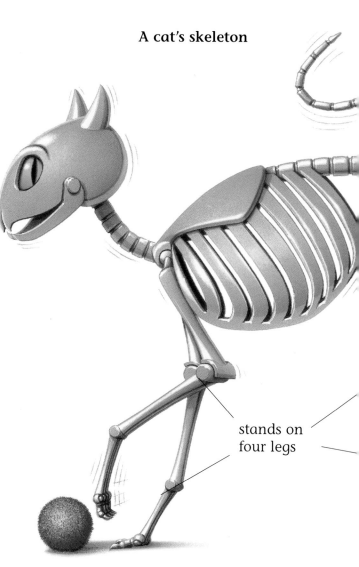

A cat's skeleton

stands on four legs

Cats

Unlike humans, cats stand on all four **limbs**. They have about 40 more bones than you do—and most of them are in their **spine**. This makes them flexible and agile. Their **coccyx** extends into a long, wavy tail, which helps them to balance as they leap around.

Snails

A snail doesn't have a skeleton under its skin. Instead it has a tough, bony shell on its back. The snail can curl up inside this, protecting its fleshy body from other animals that may want to eat it. Snails use muscles to glide slowly along the ground.

A snail

Worms

A worm has no bones at all. Its body is made of ring-like segments that stay in shape because they're full of fluid. These rings help the worm to move. They **contract** one way to make the worm's body longer and thinner. Then they pull the worm into a shorter, fatter shape, moving it along the ground.

Jellyfish

These slimy creatures are completely supported by layers of **cells** and a jellylike substance in between. They swim by expanding their bodies, then pulling them back again.

Fish

Fish have bendable spines that run from their heads to their tails. This helps them to wiggle their bodies back and forth, pushing them through the water. Instead of limbs, fish have fins. These flaps act like paddles, helping them to swim.

Insects

Insects don't have bones inside their bodies. Instead, they have a tough, ridged outer skin that bends in sections, like a suit of armor. This hard skin doesn't stretch like ours does. That's why as an insect grows, it has to shed its old skin and grow a larger one to fit its new size.

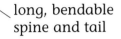

long, bendable spine and tail

Birds

Birds need bones to keep their shape—but a heavy skeleton would make it hard for them to fly. That's why a bird's bones are almost hollow, with just a few fine rods supporting them inside. This means they're fairly strong, but light enough to take to the air. Powerful muscles enable birds to flap their wings.

hollow bones are very light

strong muscles move wings

A bird's wing

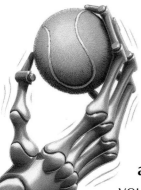

GLOSSARY

abdomen The part of your torso below your ribs.

biceps The muscle on top of your upper arm that tightens to raise your lower arm as you bend your elbow.

calcium The chalky white mineral that your bones contain to make them hard.

cartilage The slightly soft, springy material that cushions most of your joints. Cartilage also forms the more bendable parts of your skeleton, such as the ridge of your nose.

cells The billions of very tiny parts that combine to make tissues in your body.

coccyx A set of four bones that are fused together at the bottom of your spine.

collagen The protein in your bones that helps to make them strong and less brittle.

compact bone The hard, dense material that forms the outside layers of your bones.

contract To shorten and tighten. Muscles work by contracting to pull on your bones.

cramp The pain you feel when your muscles contract suddenly, tensing up.

cranium The upper part of your skull.

diaphragm The sheet of muscle below your lungs. It pushes down to make extra room for your lungs when you breathe in.

dislocate To force the bones in a joint to pop out of place.

femur The heavy bone in your thigh.

fibers Fine strands that are bundled together to form your muscles.

fibula One of the bones in your lower leg.

filaments The minute strands of protein that form your myofibrils. They slide over one another to make your muscles move.

gluteus maximus The large, rounded muscle in each buttock that you use when you sit down or stand up.

heart The organ that pumps blood around your body. Your heart is a type of muscle.

humerus The bone in your upper arm.

intercostal muscles The muscles between your ribs that move your ribcage.

joints The points where your bones meet.

lactic acid A waste product that your muscles make when you use them.

ligaments The tough cords that hold your bones together at your joints.

limbs Parts that branch out from the main torso. Your limbs are your arms and legs.

lungs The two sponge-like organs in your chest that fill with air as you breathe in.

mandible Your lower jaw bone.

marrow The soft jelly inside your bones that can make and store useful materials for your body, such as blood cells and fat.

myofibrils Tiny threads that make up each of your muscle fibers.

nutrients The chemical substances in food that your body needs to survive.

osteoarthritis A condition that many people suffer from in old age. It happens when the bones rub together at their joints, making them swollen, stiff, and painful.

oxygen A gas, found in air, that enters your body when you breathe in. Your body needs oxygen for its cells to work properly.

pelvis The heavy, bowl-shaped set of bones that makes up your bottom and hips.

processes Bony knobs that tendons hook on to, fixing your muscles to your skeleton.

protein A nutrient that your body needs to build new cells and repair itself. Protein is the main ingredient in your muscles.

radius One of your lower arm bones.

sacrum The triangular bone that joins the bottom of your spine to your pelvis.

sinuses The small spaces in your skull that make your head lighter. Sinuses are joined by openings to the airway inside your nose.

spinal cord The long bundle of nerves that runs down the center of your back, carrying messages from your brain to the rest of your body.

spine The set of bones, called vertebrae, that runs down the center of your back.

spongy bone The light material that forms the inside of your bones. It's full of little spaces, like honeycomb.

sprain To overstretch or tear the ligaments or tendons of a joint.

sternum The dagger-shaped bone that joins ten pairs of ribs at the front of your chest.

sutures Zigzag joints that lock some bones together, such as those in your skull.

synovial fluid The fluid that oils your joints.

tendons The tough strings that link your muscles to your bones.

tibia One of the bones in your lower leg.

torso The main part of your body, not including your head, neck, arms, and legs.

triceps The muscle on the underside of your upper arm, which you use to lower your forearm and straighten your elbow.

ulna One of the bones in your lower arm.

vertebrae The small, odd-shaped bones that make up your spine.

vitamin D A chemical that helps your bones to absorb and use calcium and other nutrients from your blood.

x-ray A special photograph that shows the bones inside your body.

INDEX